THE . . .
CHALDÆAN
ORACLES. .
VOL. II. . .

WORKS BY THE SAME AUTHOR

	Nd.
THRICE GREATEST HERMES (3 vols.)	30/-
FRAGMENTS OF A FAITH FORGOTTEN	10/6
DID JESUS LIVE 100 B.C. ?	9/-
THE WORLD-MYSTERY	5/-
THE GOSPEL AND THE GOSPELS	4/6
APOLLONIUS OF TYANA	3/6
THE UPANISHADS (2 vols.)	3/-
PLOTINUS	1/-

ECHOES BY
FROM G. R. S.
THE MEAD
GNOSIS VOL. IX.

THE
CHALDÆAN
ORACLES.
VOL. II.

THE LONDON
THEOSOPHICAL AND
PUBLISHING BENARES
SOCIETY 1908

The Chaldean Oracles
Volume II
First Published 1908

This reprint published 1993 by

The Banton Press
Nelson St, Largs
Scotland.

ISBN: 1 85652 132 X

ECHOES FROM THE GNOSIS.

Under this general title is now being published a series of small volumes, drawn from, or based upon, the mystic, theosophic and gnostic writings of the ancients, so as to make more easily audible for the ever-widening circle of those who love such things, some echoes of the mystic experiences and initiatory lore of their spiritual ancestry. There are many who love the life of the spirit, and who long for the light of gnostic illumination, but who are not sufficiently equipped to study the writings of the ancients at first hand, or to follow unaided the labours of scholars. These little volumes are therefore intended to serve as introduction to the study of the more difficult literature of the subject; and it is hoped that at the same time they may become for some, who have as yet not even heard of the Gnosis, stepping-stones to higher things.

G. R. S. M.

ECHOES FROM THE GNOSIS

Vol. I. THE GNOSIS OF THE MIND.
Vol. II. THE HYMNS OF HERMES.
Vol. III. THE VISION OF ARIDÆUS.
Vol. IV. THE HYMN OF JESUS.
Vol. V. THE MYSTERIES OF MITHRA.
Vol. VI. A MITHRIAC RITUAL.
Vol. VII. THE GNOSTIC CRUCIFIXION.
Vol. VIII. THE CHALDÆAN ORACLES, I.
Vol. IX. THE CHALDÆAN ORACLES, II.

PROPOSED SUBJECTS FOR FORTHCOMING VOLUMES

HYMN OF THE ROBE OF GLORY.
THE WEDDING-HYMN OF WISDOM.
SOME ORPHIC FRAGMENTS.

THE CHALDÆAN ORACLES.

VOLUME II.

CONTENTS.

FRAGMENTS AND COMMENTS— PAGE

The Starters	9
The Maintainers	18
The Enders	22
The Daimones	25
The Dogs	26
The Human Soul	30
The Vehicles of Man	32
Soul-Slavery	35
The Body	37
Nature	38
The Divine Spark	42
The Way of Return	44
The Armour of Sounding Light	45
The Way Above	50
Purification by Fire	54
The Angelic Powers of Purification	55
The Sacred Fires	57
The Fruit of the Fire Tree	60
The Pæan of the Soul	62
The Mystery-Cultus	63
The Mystic Marriage	65

The Purifying Mysteries	65
The Fire-Gnosis	67
The Manifestations of the Gods	68
The Theurgic Art	72
The Royal Souls	74
The Light-Spark	75
The Unregenerate	78
The Perfecting of the Body	80
Reincarnation	85
The Darkness	86
The Infernal Stairs	88
On Conduct	91
The Gnosis of Piety	94

BIBLIOGRAPHY.

K. = Kroll (G.), *De Oraculis Chaldaicis;* in *Breslauer philologische Abhandlungen*, Bd. vii., Hft. i. (Breslau; 1894).

C. = Cory (I. P.), *Ancient Fragments* (London; 2nd ed., 1832), pp. 239—280. The first and third editions do not contain the text of our Oracles.

F. = Mead (G. R. S.), *Fragments of a Faith Forgotten* (London; 2nd. ed., 1906).

H. = Mead (G. R. S.), *Thrice Greatest Hermes* (London; 1906).

THE CHALDÆAN ORACLES.

FRAGMENTS AND COMMENTS.

(Continued.)

THE STARTERS.

On the borderland between the intelligible and sensible worlds were the Iynges—mysterious beings whose name may perhaps be translated as Wheels or Whirls, or even as Shriekers. As, however, I seem to detect in these three ruling Principles a correspondence with the creators, preservers and destroyers, or rather regenerators (perfecters or enders) of Indian theosophy, I will call these Iynges Starters, in the sense of Initiators or Setters-up of the initial impulse.

We will first set down the "wisdom" of the lexicon on this puzzling subject,

THE CHALDÆAN ORACLES. warning the reader that he is having his attention turned to the wrong side of the thing—the littleness and superstition of what in the Oracles was clearly intended to be a revelation of some greatness.

Iynx is said to be the bird which we call the wryneck; it was called *iynx* in Greek from its cry, as it is called wryneck in English from the movement of its head. *Iygē* and *iygmós* are used of howling, shrieking, yelling, both for shouts of joy and cries of pain, and also of the hissing of snakes.

The ancient wizards, it is said, used to bind the wryneck to a wheel, which they made to revolve, in the belief that they thus drew men's hearts along with it and chained them to obedience; hence this magic wheel was frequently used in the belief that it was a means of recovering unfaithful lovers. This operation was called setting the magic bird or magic wheel agoing. The unfortunate bird seems to have been attached to the wheel with its wings and legs pegged out crosswise so as to form four spokes, spread-eagle fashion. The word *iynx* thus came to mean a charm, and a spell, and also a passionate yearning.

The root-idea accordingly seems to have been that of a " winged wheel " that emitted sound, and we are reminded of the winged creatures or wheels in the famous Vision of Ezekiel, who saw the mystic sight in Babylon, and thus probably caught some reflection of the symbolism of the Chaldæan mysteries.

How the wryneck was first brought in, and finally assumed the chief place, is a puzzle. It reminds one of the story of the calf in the Vaidik rite, which so interfered with the sacred service of the sage that he had to tie it up to a post before he could continue the rite. This casual incident became finally sterotyped into the chief feature of the rite !

Certain it is that the Iynges of our Oracles have nothing to do with wrynecks ; we shall, therefore, make bold to translate them as Wheels or Starters.

THE CHALDÆAN ORACLES. They were presumably thought of as Living Spheres, whirling out in every direction from the centre, and swirling in again to that same centre, once they had reached the limit of their periphery or surround. They were also, in all probability, conceived of as Winged Globes—a familiar figure in Babylonian and Egyptian art—thus symbolizing that they were powers of the Air, midway between Heaven, the Great Surround, and Earth, the fixed Centre. In other words, they were the Children of the Æon.

An anonymous ancient writer tells us (K. 39) that it is the blending of the intellectual (or gnostic) and intelligible (or ideal) orders—that is, the union of the prototypes of what we distinguish as subject and object in the sense-world of diversity, or what we might call the self-reflective energy of the Mind on the plane of reality—that first "spirts forth" the One Iynx, and after this the three Iynges that are called "paternal" and also "unspeakables." This writer also characterizes the Iynx as the "One in the three Depths after it" (it is, therefore, of an æonic nature), and says that it is this three-in-one hierarchy that divides the worlds into three—namely, empyrean, ætherial, and terrene.

The information of Damascius refines and complicates the idea, when he tells us that "the Mind of the Father is said to bring forward [on to the stage of manifestation] the triadic ordering—Iynges, Synoches, Teletarchæ"—which we may render tentatively as Whirlings, Holdings-together and Perfectings.

The Synoches we have come across before (i. 58). *Teletarchía* is used by ecclesiastical writers as a synonym of the Trinity; while Orpheus is called *teletárchēs* as the founder of mysteries or perfectionings.

The root-meanings underlying the names of the members of this triad seem to suggest, as we have already said, the ideas of creating (or preferably starting), preserving (or maintaining), and completing (or perfecting or finishing).

Damascius thinks that the last words of the following two verses refer to the triad of the One Iynx.

K. 40.
C. 40.
Many are these who leaping mount upon the shining worlds; among them are three excellencies [or *heights*].

The meaning of the first clause is doubtful. Who the many (fem. pl.) are, is not clear; it may mean that there are hosts of subordinate Iynges. On the contrary, it may have nothing to do with these Nature-Iynges on the Path of Descent, that is the bringing into manifestation, but may refer to souls who in the Ascent win their way to the "shining worlds" or Worlds of Light, and become Iynges consciously

According to both Damascius and Proclus, the Order of Iynges is characterized as having the power both of proceeding or going-forth and of drawing-together or contracting—that is, both of expansion and contraction, of out-breathing and in-breathing. They are, moreover, free Intelligences.

The Whirls [Iynges] created by the Father's Thought are themselves, too, intelligent [or gnostic], being moved by Wills ineffable to understand.

K. 40.
C. 54.

They are created by Divine Thought, as Sons of Will and Yoga, and procreate by thought; they are Mind-born and give birth to minds. Their epithet is the "*Ineffables*" or "*Unspeakables*"; they are further called in the Oracles "*swift*," and are said to proceed from and to "*rush to*" or "*desire eagerly*" the Father (C. 52); they are the "*Father's Powers*." Indeed, as Proclus declares:

" For not only do these three divinities [or divine natures] of themselves bring into manifestation and contract them [*sci.*, out of manifestation], but they are

THE CHALDÆAN ORACLES. also '*Guardians*' [or Watchers or Preservers] of the '*works*' of the Father, according to the Oracle—yea, of the One Mind that doth create itself" (K. 40, C. 41).

Iynx in its root-meaning, according to Proclus, signifies the "power of transmission," which is said, in the Oracles, "*to sustain the fountains.*" The same idea seems to be latent in the following verse:

K. 40.
C. 64.
For all cosmos has inflexible intelligent sustainers.

The meaning is quite clearly brought out when Proclus, elsewhere, affirms that the Order of the Iynges "has a transmissive [that is, intermediary or ferrying] power, as the Theologers call it, of all things from the Intelligible [or Typal] Order into Matter, and again of all things into it [*sci.*, the Intelligible]."

In other words, they are the direct link between the Divine and physical, and to some extent also suggest the idea of Angels or Messengers; yet are they like to Wheels and Whirls, or Vortices—on the one hand to vortical atoms, and on the other to individualities. They are, of course, in essence, quite unbound by ideas of extension in space, and sequence in time; though they manifest in space and time.

Porphyry preserves a curious Oracle which reads:

With secret rites drawing the iynx *from the æther.*   K. 41.

This Oracle, however, may have been taken from some Theurgist or Hellenized Magian source and not from our poem; and so also may the following quoted by Proclus:

Be active [or *operate*] *round the Hecatic spinning thing.*   K. 41. C. 194.

It is doubtful what *stróphalus* means

THE CHALDÆAN ORACLES.

exactly. It may sometimes mean a top; and in the Mysteries tops were included among the mystic play-things of the young Bacchus, or Iacchus. They represented, among other things, the " fixed " stars (humming tops) and planets (whipping tops).

The Iynx was said to be active, or to energize, on the three—empyrean, ætherial and terrene—planes.

THE MAINTAINERS.

Though the Later Platonic commentators make two other allied hierarchies out of the Synoches and Teletarchæ, both these, as we have seen, should rather be taken as modes of this same mysterious Iynx. In manifestation, from one it passed to three, and so became many. Thus a scrap of our Oracles reads:

K. 41.
C. 57.

Nay, and as many as are subject to the hylic [or *terrene*] *Synoches.*

This would seem to mean simply the

Powers that hold together, or con-tract, or mass, material things; and these Powers are again the Iynges, or simultaneously creative, preservative, and destructive or perfective Intelligences of the Father-Mind, which are in the Oracles symbolically called His "*Lightnings*" when thought of as Rays or Intelligences. The word *Prēstēres* (Lightnings), however, is more graphically and literally rendered as Fiery Whirlwinds—like waterspouts. These are again our Iynges or Whirls or Swirls or Wheels, spinning in and out. Thus two verses read:

But to the Knowing Fire-whirls of the Knowing Fire [i.e., *the Father*] *all things do yield, subject unto the Father's Will which makes them to obey.*

K. 42.
C. 63.

As we have seen above (p. 16) these Whirls, as Synoches—that is, in their power of holding together—were called "Guardians," and this is borne out by two verses:

K. 42.   *He gave to His own Fire-whirls the*
C. 56.   *power to guard the summits, commingling with the Synoches the proper power of His own Might.*

    The "summits" suggest these self-same Iynges in their creative mode; the series of which they were the "summits" being creative (or inceptive), preservative (or guardian), and perfective (consummative or regenerative).

    Thus Damascius tells us that the whole Demiurgic Order—that is to say, the order of things in genesis—was surrounded by what the Oracles call the "*Fire-whirling Guard.*" In brief it is the power of holding together (? gravitation on the life-side of things).

    This is fundamentally the great power of the Mother-side of things; for, as we have seen (i. 57), the Great Mother is:

K. 19.   *Source of all sources, Womb that holds*
C. 99.   *all things together.*

It follows, therefore, that the Iynges, as creative, are on the Father-side; as preservative (or Synoches) on the Mother-side; and as result or consummating or perfecting (or Teletarchæ) on the Son-side.

Damascius bears this out when he tells us that the Oracles call the Synoches the "*Whole-makers*" (*holopoioi*)—that is to say, they are connected with the idea of wholeness or oneness or the root-substance side of things, and again with the idea of the Æon.

Of course, the symbolic categories of Father, Mother, and Son are really all aspects of One and the same Mystery—the That which understands itself alone and yet is beyond understanding. To this Proclus refers when he writes (K. 42, C. 7): "Including [containing, preserving] all things in the one excellency [or summit] of His own subsistence, '*Himself subsists wholly beyond*,' according to the Oracle."

THE ENDERS.

So also with the Teletarchæ or Perfecting Powers; as Proclus tells us, they have the same divisions as the Synoches (and Iynges); that is to say, it is again all the same thing looked at from the Son-side of things. There was thus, in the elaboration of the Later Platonic commentators, a triple, and even a sevenfold, division of this order or hierarchy. Considering the Teletarchic energy, or activity, as triadic, Proclus tells us that in its first mode it has to do with the finest or ultimate substance, the Empyrean, and says that it plays the part of Driver or Guide to the "*foot* [?—tarsón] *of Fire*"—which may be simply a poetical phrase for the Fire in its first contact with substance. Its middle mode, embracing beginnings and ends and middles, perfects the Æther; while its third mode is concerned with Gross Matter (*Hylē*), still confused and unshaped, which it also perfects.

From these and other elaborations of a like nature, we learn that the Teletarchs were regarded as three, and were intimately bound up with the Synoches, and therefore with the Iynges (C. 58). The unifying or holding-together of the Synochic power is de-fined and de-limited by the perfecting nature of the Teletarchic power—

THE CHALDÆAN ORACLES.

Into beginning and end and middle things by Order of Necessity.

K. 43.

In this connection it is of interest to cite a sentence from Proclus that is almost certainly quoted from the Oracles. It relates to the Ascent of the individual soul and not to cosmogenesis, to perfection in the Mysteries and not to the Mysteries that perfect the world :

The Soul-lord, he who doth set his feet upon the realms ætherial, is the Perfectioner [*Teletarch*].

K. 43.

Finally, Proclus refers the following two verses to the Teletarchs :

K. 43. *Nay, a Name of august majesty, and,*
C. 111. *with sleepless whirling, leaping into the worlds, by reason of the Father's swift Announcement.*

In another passage Proclus refers to the "*Transmissive*" Name that leaps into activity in the "*boundless worlds*" (K. 44); and in yet another passage (K. 40), which we have already quoted (p. 16), he gives this "Name" to the Iynges. This plainly refers to the "*Intermediaries who stand*" between the Father and Matter, as Damascius says (K. 44), who further affirms that in their aspect of Teletarchs they are perfecting, and rule over all perfections, or the perfecting rites of the Mysteries.

So much, then, for the highest Principles or Ruling Powers of the Sensible World. The commentators further speak of a division among the Gods into Gods within the Zones and Gods beyond the Zones; but no verse from the Oracles is extant by which we can control this statement. It seems to mean simply that they were classified according as to whether their operations were concerned with the Seven Spheres, or were beyond them.

THE CHALDÆAN ORACLES.

THE DAIMONES.

The lesser powers were, according to Olympiodorus, divided into Angels, Daimones and Heroes. Concerning the Heroes, however, we have no fragment remaining ; while Angels and Daimones are at times somewhat confused. On the Daimones we have the following two verses :

Nature persuades us that the Daimones are pure, and things that grow from evil matter useful and good.

K. 44.
C. 191.

Kroll thinks that this means that Nature deceives us into thinking that the evil Daimones are good ; it may, however, mean that whereas from Man's standpoint Daimones are good or evil,

THE CHALDÆAN ORACLES. according to Nature they are pure, or indifferent, or non-moral. Their operations are conditioned by man's nature. They are in themselves non-human entities, and there is a scale of them from lowest to highest.

THE DOGS.

Certain classes of them the Oracles call "*Dogs*"; and here we may quote an interesting passage from Lydus (K. 30):

"Whence the tradition of the Mystic Discourse [? the Oracles] that Hecatē [the World-Mother] is four-headed because of the four elements. And the fire-breathing head of the Horse evidently refers as it were to the sphere of fire; the bellowing head of the Bull has reference to a certain bellowing power connected with the sphere af air; the bitter and unstable nature of the Hydra [or Water-serpent] is connected with the sphere of water; and the chastening and avenging nature of the Dog with that of earth."

The last clause throws some light on the allied figure of Anubis in Egyptian psychopompy, and also on the following fragment of the Oracles:

THE CHALDÆAN ORACLES.

Out of the Womb of Earth leap Dogs terrestrial that unto mortal never show true sign.

K. 45.
C. 97.

It is impossible to say what this means precisely without the context. "Dogs" are the intelligent guardians of the secrets of various mystery-traditions; they are ever watchful. The Outer Guards of the Adyta in which the mystic rites were celebrated, were sometimes called Dogs. Much could be written on this symbolism, beginning with Anubis and the Dog-ape of Thoth (see "Dog" in the Index of *H*.). Dog was a name of honour in the Mysteries. The Pythagoræans called the Planets the "Dogs of Persephonē"; sparks were poetically called the "Dogs of Hephæstus." The Eumenides, were called "Dogs," and the Harpies "Dogs

THE CHALDÆAN ORACLES. of Great Zeus." Perhaps this may throw some light on our particular Oracle; in the Oracles generally, however, they seem to have been a generic name of apparently wider meaning than in the symbolism which Lydus uses; unless we assume that for him the earth-sphere extended to the moon, when it would have three "planes"—terrene, watery and aëry—each of which had its appropriate Dogs.

Thus Olympiodorus writes: "From the aëry spaces begin to come into existence the irrational Daimones. Wherefore also the Oracle says:"

K. 45.
C. 75.
She [? Hecatē] is the Driver of the aëry and the earthy and the watery Dogs.

Kroll refers to the last of these Dogs the epithet "*Water-walkers,*" which Proclus quotes from the Oracles in the following passage:

"'Watery' as applied to divine natures signifies the undivided domain over water; for which cause, too, the Oracle calls these Gods '*Water-walkers*'" (K. 45, C. 76).

It is clear, however, that this refers to a far higher "dominion" than that of the Dogs. These inferior Daimones had their existence as far as the Moon only, in what was regarded as the realm of the impure nature or gross matter. Beyond the Moon the Daimones were held to be of a higher and purer order; these were also called Angels—a term that in all probability came into our Hellenized Oracles along the line of the Mago-Chaldæan tradition.

Psellus speaks of "*the manifoldly-flowing tribes*" (the group-soul idea) of the Daimones, and this phrase was in all probability taken from the Oracles. (K. 46). It would seem to indicate that the nature of the Daimones was unstable and Protean, or rather that they could assume any form at will.

THE HUMAN SOUL.

We now come to the important subject of the doctrine of the Oracles concerning the human soul.

The soul, as we have already seen (i. 71), was brought into being by the union of three ; it is a triad, or rather a monad united with a triad.

K. 26.
C. 81.
Having mingled the Spark of soul with two in unanimity—with Mind and Breath Divine—to them He added, as a third, Pure Love, the august Master binding all.

We must, then, suppose that the individual souls, as lives, flow forth from the World-Soul, the Great Mother ; it is, however, the Father who conditions them by His Creative Thought.

K. 46.
C. 78.
These things the Father thought, and [so] made mortal [man] to be ensouled.

"Mortal man" here seems to mean man as conditioned by body. The Soul is, as it were, a middle term between Mind and Body—both for the Great World and for the little world, or man; for two verses run:

The Father of men and gods placed Mind in Soul, and Soul in inert Body. K. 47.
C. 18.

The fundamental distinction, however, between the Mind and Soul is not easy to draw with any great clearness. They may be thought of as Light and Life, the eternally united complements of the One Mystery, the masculine and feminine powers of the sexless Supreme. So also with the individual soul in man; the soul-spark is a light-spark which is also a life-spark, or rather life-flood; it is centre and sphere in perpetual embrace —for mind and soul are not to be separated, no man can put them asunder. The nature of this "soul" (*ātma-buddhi*) is immortal and divine.

K. 47. *For Soul being shining Fire, by reason*
C. 20. *of the Father's Power, both keeps immune*
from Death, and body is of Life, and hath
the fulnesses [plērōmata] *of many wombs.*

In the cosmic process (and also in the case of the individual) when the Sea of Substance has been impregnated by the Beams of Light, the whole Sea changes from dull and sluggish Matter (*tamas*) to bright Soul (*sattva*). It has become one now instead of indeterminate, cosmic and no longer chaotic. It is now the Sea of Life, the complement of all imperfection.

It is in all probability to the individual Soul that Psellus refers, when he writes : " For if, according to the Oracles, it is ' *a portion of the Fire Divine,*' and ' *shining Fire,*" and ' *a creation of the Father's Thought,*' its form is immaterial and self-subsistent " (K. 47, n. 2).

THE VEHICLES OF MAN.

The original text of our Oracle-poem had, probably, something to tell us of other "vehicles" or "garments" of the Soul besides the gross body; but no verses on this interesting subject are extant. THE CHALDÆAN ORACLES.

Proclus, however, tells us that the disciples of Porphyry "seem to follow the Oracles, in saying that in its Descent the Soul 'collects a portion of Æther and of Sun and Moon, and all the elements contained in Air.'" Compare with this the Oracle quoted above (i. 79):

O Æther, Sun, Moon's Breath, Leaders of Air.   K. 33.
C. 136.

And also a fragment of Porphyry preserved by Stobæus:
"For when the soul goes forth from the solid body, there follows along with it the spirit which it collected from the spheres" (K. 47, n. 3).

And with this compare the following passage from the Trismegistic tractate "The Key":

"Now the principles of man are this wise vehicled: mind in the reason, the

THE CHALDÆAN ORACLES.

reason in the soul, soul in the spirit, and spirit in the body.

"Spirit pervading body, by means of veins and arteries and blood, bestows upon the living creature motion, and, as it were, doth bear it in a way. . . .

"It is the same for those who go out from the body.

"For when the soul withdraws into itself, the spirit doth contract within the blood, and soul within the spirit. And then the mind, stripped of its wrappings, and naturally divine, takes to itself a fiery body" (*H.*, ii. 149, 151).

And so also Proclus, treating of the Ascent or Return, and plainly referring to the Oracles, writes:

"In order that both the visible vehicle may, through the visible action of them [*sci.*, the Rays], obtain its proper treatment [or care], and that the vehicle that's more divine than this, may secretly be purified, and [so] return to its own proper lot, '*drawn upward by the lunar and the solar Rays,'* as says somewhere one of the Gods [*i.e.*, the Oracles]."

Compare with this the Pitṛi-yāna and Deva-yāna, or Way of the Fathers and Way of the Gods, in the Upaniṣhads. This " more divine vehicle " was generally called by the Later Platonic school the " ray-like " (*augo-eidés*), or " star-like " (*astro-eidés*), or " spirituous " (*pneumatikón*) body; and its purification and enlivening by means of the Rays are admirably set forth in the rubrics of the *Mithriac Ritual* (Vol. VI.).

SOUL-SLAVERY.

In itself, the Soul is possessed of a divine nature, and is naturally free; in the earth-state, however, it is now in slavery owing to its being drunk with the things of gross matter (*hylē*). This at any rate seems to be the meaning of the following three lines that have, unfortunately, been considerably mangled by the copyists:

K. 48.   *The Soul of man shall press God closely*
C. 83.   *to itself, with naught subject to death in it ; [but now] it is all drunk, for it doth glory in the Harmony beneath whose sway the mortal frame exists*

With these lines are probably to be taken the verse quoted above (i. 30) :

K. 15.   *Not knowing God is wholly God. O*
C. 184.   *wretched slaves, be sober!*

The Harmony is the system of the Seven Formative Spheres of Genesis, or Fate. And so Proclus, speaking of Souls, writes :

" Which also the Gods [*i.e.*, the Oracles] say are slaves when they turn to generation (*genesis*) ; but '*if they serve their slavery with neck unbent*,' they are brought home again from out this state, leaving the state of birth-and-death (*genesis*) behind."

THE BODY.

As to body, the doctrine of the Oracles was, as with nearly all the mystic schools of the time, that of naïve ascetic dualism in general, that is if we can trust the commentators. Body seems more or less to have been identified with matter. It is said to be "in a state of flux," "spread out," and "scattered." It was apparently called, in the Oracles, the "*tumultuous vessel*" or "*vessel of tumult*"—the epithet being derived from rushing, roaring and dashing waves, and the idea being connected with the flowing nature of material things, presumably, as contrasted with the quiet of the contemplative mind.

Proclus speaks of "the earth from which one must '*lighten the heart*'" (K. 48), and this "heart" must be associated with what he calls, after the Oracles, "the '*inner heart*' in the essence of the soul" (K. 47, n. 1).

The unfortunate body is thus regarded as the "*root of evil*," or "*naughtiness*,"

THE CHALDÆAN ORACLES. and is said to be even the "*purgation of matter*" (K. 48), one of our extant fragments characterizing it plainly as the "*dung*" or "*dross of matter*" (K. 61, C. 147).

It may here be noted that in the *Pistis Sophia*, matter is called the "superfluity of naughtiness," and men (that is men's bodies) are said to be the "purgation of the matter (*hylē*) of the Rulers" (*P.S.*, 249, 251, 337); and it is very credible that this was one of the doctrines of the "Books of the Chaldæans."

Matter (*hylē*) is here not regarded as the fruitful substance of the universe, the "Land flowing with milk and honey," but as the dry and squalid element beneath the Moon, which, Proclus tells us, is called, in the Oracles, the "*un-watered*," that is in itself unfruitful, the Desert as compared with the Land of true living substance (K. 48).

NATURE.

In this gross matter dwells the body which is subject to Nature, that is Fate.

The physical body, then, appears to have been regarded as an excretion within the domain of Nature or the Fate-sphere. Psellus, accordingly, writes concerning the Soul, or rather the Light-spark:

"But the Gnostic Fire comes from Above, and is in need of its native Source alone [presumably, the true spiritual life-substance]; but if it be affected by the feelings of the body, Necessity compels that it should serve it [the body] and [so] be set beneath the sway of Fate, and led about by Nature" (K. 48).

This suggests the putting on the "form of a servant," of the Pauline Letters (*Phil.*, ii. 7), and the Trismegistic "becoming a slave within the Harmony [*i.e.*, Fate-sphere]" (*H.*, ii. 10).

This gross matter, or hylic substance, extended as far as the Moon; it constituted, therefore, practically the atmosphere, or surround, of the earth, generally spoken of as the sublunary region. The Moon was its "Ruler," being the "image" of the Great Mother, Nature, who conditions

THE CHALDÆAN ORACLES. all genesis—that is, becoming or birth-and-death. Speaking of this Lunar Sphere, which surrounds the hylic regions, Proclus tells us that in it were " the causes of all genesis " or generation; and quotes a sacred *logos* in confirmation :

K. 49. *The self-revealed glory* [or *image*] *of Nature shines forth.*

Whether these words are quoted directly from our poem, is not quite certain ; it is, however, highly probable, for an isolated verse runs :

K. 49.
C. 148. *Do not invoke the self-revealed image of Nature.*

Here Mother Nature is what the Greeks called Hecatē, and her " image " or nature-symbol, or glory, is the Moon. Very similar to this is the fragment :

K. 49.
C. 149. *Turn not thy face Naturewards* ; [*for*] *her Name is identical with Fate.*

Perhaps the second clause has been defaced in the tradition; it is difficult to make out the precise sense from the present text, unless it means simply, as Iamblichus tells us, that: "The whole being [or essence] of Fate is in Nature"—that is to say, that Nature and Fate are identical.

In close connection with this we must take the Oracular prohibition:

Do not increase thy Fate! K. 50.
C. 153.

Fate may here be said to be the result of contact with many people and objects. Everything that we have intercourse with on earth enlarges our destiny, for destiny in this sense is the result of earthly happenings. We should, accordingly, seek within everything for further ideas, and not simply rush about and spread ourselves all over space. This seeking within by means of true mind is not stirring up the secret powers of Great Nature; it is rather the understanding of Fate.

THE CHALDÆAN ORACLES.

The prohibition thus seems to mean: Do not increase the dominion of the body of the lower nature, or rather the Moon-ruled plasm.

Within the same range of ideas also, we may, perhaps, bring the isolated apostrophe from the Oracles:

K. 50.
C. 94.
O man, thou subtle handiwork of daring Nature!

This refers to the body of man that is wrought by the Nature-powers, the elemental intelligences of the Mother.

THE DIVINE SPARK.

The "soul" is thus thought of, in this doctrine, as struggling against the "body"; in this great Struggle, or Passion, it is helped by the Father, who has bestowed upon it a particle, or rather portion, of His own Mind, the living "*symbol*," or pledge, or token, of Himself. This struggle, or passion, is in reality the travail, or birth-throes, of the self-born Son. It is because of this Light-spark, by reason of this pledge, that souls fallen into generation, and therefore forgetful in time of their Divine origin, can recover the memory of the Father.

For the Mind of the Father hath sown symbols through the world—[the Mind] that understands things understandable, and that thinks-forth ineffable beauties.   K. 50.
C. 47.

Psellus has a variant of the first verse, namely:

The Mind of the Father has sown symbols in the souls.   C. 80.

These "symbols" are the seeds of Divinity (the *logoi* or "words" of Philo and the Christian Gnosis), but they are not operative until the soul converts its will from the things of Fate to those of Freedom, from self-will to spiritual free-will. On this we have, fortunately, three verses preserved:

K. 50.　　*But the Mind of the Father doth not*
C. 164.　　*receive her will, until she hath departed
from Oblivion, and uttereth the word, by
putting in its [Oblivion's] place the Memory
of the Fatherhood's pure token.*

On this Psellus comments: "Each, therefore, diving into the ineffable depths of his own nature, findeth the symbol of the All-Father." "Uttering the word" is, mystically, bringing this *logos*, or light-spark, into activity.

THE WAY OF RETURN.

The Path of Return to the Father was set forth at length in the Oracles, and on it we have, fortunately, a number of fragments:

K. 51.　　*Seek out the channel of the Soul-stream,*
C. 172.　　*—whence and from what order is it that
the soul in slavery to body [did descend,
and] to what order thou again shalt rise,
at-one-ing work with holy word.*

44

The meaning of "word" in this and the preceding fragment is doubtful. We may either take it mystically, as we have suggested above, or it may be taken magically, as the utterance of compelling speech—in the lower sense, the theurgic use of invocations, and in the higher the utterance of true "words of power," that is the "speech of the gods" which is uttered by right action, or "work." This reminds us of the "Great Work" of the Alchemists, and of Karma-yoga, or the "union by works," of Vaidik theosophy, taken in the mystic sense and not the usual meaning of ceremonial acts. Kroll thinks that the "holy word" means the knowledge of the intelligible world of the Father, but I do not quite follow him.

THE ARMOUR OF SOUNDING LIGHT.

The nature of the Quest is set forth mysteriously as follows:

Armed at all points, clad in the bloom of Sounding Light, arming both mind and   K. 51.
C. 170.

soul with three-barbed Might, he must set in his heart the Triad's every symbol, and not move scatteredly along the empyrean ways [or *channels*], *but* [*move*] *collectedly.*

Compare with this (i. 87):

K. 36.　*Yea, verily, full-armed without and*
C. 171.　*armed within like to a goddess.*

This refers to the Re-generate, as described in the *Mithriac Ritual*. The "three-barbed Might" is taken probably from the symbol of the trident, and represents the triple-power of the Monad. As the *Ritual* says (page 27), he must hold himself steady and not allow himself to be "scattered abroad"; all his "limbs" must be collected, or gathered together, as the Osiris in resurrection. Compare with this *The Gnostic Crucifixion* (pp. 16, 52 ff.), and also the remarkable description of a somewhat similar experience in a story, by E. R. Innes, in *The*

Theosophical Review (vol. xli., p. 343., Dec., 1907).

Especially to be noticed is the graphic phrase "Sounding Light," showing that the close connection between colour and sound was known to the initiates of these mysteries. This Sounding Light, however, in its mystical sense, was probably the Uttered Word, or, to use another figure, the putting-on of the "Robe of Glory." Compare with this the Descent of the Eagle in the Hymn of the Soul of Bardaisan :

" It flew in the form of the Eagle,
   Of all the winged tribes the king-bird;
It flew and alighted beside me,
   And turned into speech altogether."
                        (*F.*, p. 410).

This Sounding Light is thus the true "symbol" of the Paternal or Spiritual or Intelligible Monad. Proclus speaks of the intelligence as being "well-wheeled," by which he means smoothly spinning round a centre; this centre

THE CHALDÆAN ORACLES. being the Intelligible (K. 51). But, to our taste, this is by no means a good simile, for the Intelligible or Spiritual Mind embraces all things and is not a centre. Proclus, however, seems to base himself upon this verse:

K. 51.
C. 126.
Urging himself to the centre of Sounding Light.

But when we remember the "three-barbed Might" of our first fragment above (K. 51, C. 170), we may, perhaps, be permitted to translate *kéntron* as "goad":

Urging himself on with the goad of Sounding Light.

We thus bring the main idea into relation with the contemporaneous Trismegistic doctrine of the Master-Mind (*i.e.*, the Spiritual Mind) being the Charioteer, and driving the soul-chariot, with gnostic rays (or reins) that sound forth its true counsels. In any case the mystic should find no difficulty in transmuting the symbols, passing from centre to periphery or from periphery to centre as the thought requires.

Finally, with regard to the first quotation under this heading, it may be said that in re-generation man begins to re-clothe himself; only when he makes these new clothes, they no longer bind but clothe him with power. The "bloom" (or vigour) of Sounding (or Resounding) Light is an armour that rays forth. "Might" (or Strength) suggests inner stability, that which is planted within and is the root of stability, the foundation. The ātmic, or spiritual, "spark," in the virgin soil, or womb, of the man's spiritual nature, is the Strength of the Father. It is the Power to stop chaos swirling, and so start the enforming or ordering of itself. Thus it is that the man starts making the symbols and sounds whereby his Name or Word is actualized.

THE WAY ABOVE.

Such a man should begin to know the nature of the regions unto which he is being brought, and so understand the mystic precept :

K. 51.
C. 174.

Let the immortal depths of thy soul be opened, and open all thy eyes at once to the Above.

It is proper to follow the "great" passions and desires of the soul, provided the "eye," or true centre of the mind, be fixed Above ; for then the passions are sure to be pure, and not personal attractions, not little bonds of feeling and sentiment.

This "opening of all the eyes" concerns the mystery of the Æon. In the Depths of the New Dawn every atom of the man must become an eye ; he must be "all eye." As vehicle of Sounding Light he must become an Æon—"a Star in the world of men, an Eye in the regions of the gods."

But to be clothed with this Royal Vesture, this Robe of Glory, he must strip off the "garb of the servant," the bonds of slavery, the "earthy carapace":

The mortal once endowed with Mind must on his soul put bridle, in order that it may not plunge into the ill-starred Earth but win to freedom.

K. 52.
C. 175.

"Endowed with Mind" is the Trismegistic "Mind-led." This Spiritual Mind, or Great Mind, is the Promethean, or Foreseeing, Mind in man (as Proclus tells us), who plays the part of Providence over the life of reason in us—that is, the rational man or animal—that this life may not be destroyed by being—

Dowsed in the frenzies of the Earth and the necessities of Nature.

C. 190.

This is quoted by Proclus from our poem, for he adds: "As one of the Oracles says."

This "dowsing," or baptism, of the

THE CHALDÆAN ORACLES. soul in the waves of the Ocean of Genesis, or Generation, the Watery Spheres, is referred to several times in the Trismegistic fragments (K. 52, n. 1), and is the converse of the Spiritual Baptism or "Dowsing in the Mind," as we read in the Divine Herald's Proclamation, in the treatise called "The Cup" or "Mixing-bowl"—the Monad.

"Baptize thyself with this Cup's Baptism, what heart can do so, thou that hast faith thou canst ascend to Him who hath sent down the Cup, thou that dost know for what thou did'st come into being" (*H.*, ii. 87).

Of similar purport are the verses:

K. 52.
C. 160.

Unto the Light and to the Father's Rays thou ought'st to hasten, whence hath been sent to thee a soul richly with Mind arrayed.

"Hasten" is a mystery-word, suggesting activity without motion. The soul must be lightened and stripped of its gross garments of matter (*hylē*).

For things Divine are not accessible to mortals who fix their minds on body; 'tis they who strip them naked [of this thing], that speed aloft unto the Height.

K. 52.
C. 169.

These are the true Naked, the real Gymnosophists, as Apollonius of Tyana would have called them, who strip off the "form of the servant," the rags of the lower nature. Compare with this the early Jewish commentator in the Naassene Document, who was evidently well versed in the "Books of the Chaldæans":

"For this Mystery is the Gate of Heaven, and this is the House of God, where the Good God dwells alone; into which House no impure man shall come. But it is kept under watch for the Spiritual alone; where, when they come, they must cast away their garments, and all become bridegrooms, obtaining their true manhood through the Virginal Spirit" (*H.*, i. 181).

If this transmutation be effected, and

THE
CHALDÆAN
ORACLES.
the "rags" changed into the shining garments of the pure elements, the "wedding garments" of the Gospel parables, the soul by its own power wins its freedom. Such a man is characterized by Proclus as "having a soul that looks down upon body, and is capable of looking Above, '*by its own might*,' according to the Oracle, divorced from the hylic organs of sense" (K. 52).

PURIFICATION BY FIRE.

The Path of Return, or Way Above, was conceived as a purification of the soul from the hylic elements, and therewith an entry into the purifying mystery of the Baptism of Fire, which in its highest sense is the "Dowsing" in the Divine Mind of the Trismegistic teaching.

K. 53.   *For if the mortal draw nigh to the Fire,*
C. 158. *he shall have Light from God.*

Speaking of the "perfecting purification," Proclus tells us that it was operated by means of the "*Divine Fire*," and that it was the highest degree of purification, which caused all the "*stains*" that dimmed the pure nature of the soul, through her converse with generation, to disappear. This he takes directly from the Oracles.

THE ANGELIC POWERS OF PURIFICATION.

In this purification certain Divine Powers, or Intelligences, take part; they are called Angels (Messengers or Mediators). They are the higher correspondence of the infernal Daimones in *The Vision of Aridæus* (pp. 33 ff.), in which the "stains" of the souls are graphically depicted.

The part played by these Intelligences, however, is not external to the soul, but an integral part of the transmutation; it is the Angelic portion of the man that leads the soul Above.

It is this, as Proclus tells us, from the

THE CHALDÆAN ORACLES. Oracles, that "*makes*" the soul "*to shine with Fire*"—that is, which itself shines round the man on all sides; it rays-forth, becomes truly "astral" (*augo-eidés* or *astro-eidés*), rays-forth with intelligence.

It is this Angelic power that purifies the soul of gross matter (*hylē*), and "*lightens it with warm spirit*"—that is, endows it with a true impersonal or "cosmic" subtle vehicle, tempered by means of that "temperature" or "blend" which the *Mithriac Ritual* (p. 19) tells us depends entirely on the Fire.

The original poem seems, from Proclus' comments, further to have contained verses which referred to certain Angelic Powers who, as it were, made to indraw the external protrusions of the soul which it sympathetically projects in conformity with the configuration of the limbs of its earthy prison-house; their function, therefore, was to restore it to its pure spherical shape. To this may refer the very corrupt and obscure verse:

The projections of the soul are easy to unloose by being inbreathed. K. 53. C. 88.

THE SACRED FIRES.

Breath (Spirit) is said mystically to be the Spouse of Fire (Mind); and so we find Proclus speaking of " perfecting the travail of souls and '*lighting up the Fire*' in them," and also of "lighting up the fires that lead them Home"; all of which, for the mystic, can refer to nothing else than the starting of what are called the "sacred fires" of spiritual transformation. These "fires" are intelligent transforming currents that re-form the soul-plasm into the "perfect body," that is, the "body of resurrection," as the *Mithriac Ritual* (p. 19) informs us. And so we read:

Extend on every side the reins of Fire to [guide] the unformed soul. K. 53. C. 173.

That is, constrain the flowing watery nature of the soul by the fiery breath or spirit of the true Mind. And this seems

THE CHALDÆAN ORACLES. also to be the meaning of the difficult fragment:

K. 54.
C. 176.
If thou extendest fiery Mind to flowing work of piety, thou shall preserve thy body too.

This seems to mean that, when by means of purification, and by dint of pious practices, the soul is made fluid—that is to say, is no longer bound to any configuration of external things, when it is freed from prejudice, or opinion, and personal passion, or sentiment, and is " with pure purities now purified," as the *Mithriac Ritual* (p. 20) has it—then this re-generated soul-plasm, the germ of the " perfect body," can be configured afresh according to the plans or symbols of the true Mind.

Then shall the re-generate souls have Gnosis of the Divine Mind, be free from Fate, and breathe the Intelligible Fire, thus understanding the Works of the Father.

They flee the reckless fated wing of Fate, and stay themselves in God, drawing unto themselves the Fires in all their prime, as they descend from out the Father, from which, as they descend, the soul doth cull the Flower of Empyrean Fruit that nourisheth the soul.

K. 54.
C. 90.

It is hazardous to say what this may mean with any great precision, for in all probability the text is corrupt in several places. Taking it as it stands, however, we may conjecture that the first line refers to the state of the souls in subjection to Fate; they are figured elsewhere as leaving the state of sameness and rest, and flying forth down into the hylic realms of Genesis, or repeated birth and death. This is winging the " shameless " (or reckless) " wing of Fate ;" and yet this too is " fated." They who return to the memory of their spiritual state, once more rest in God, and breathe in the " Gnostic Fires " of the Holy Spirit—the true Ambrosia, that which bestows immortality (*athanasía*).

THE FRUIT OF THE FIRE-TREE.

This Fruit of Life—that is, the Gnosis, or Gnostic Son of God—as may be seen from *The Great Announcement*, of the Simonian tradition, based on Mago-Chaldæan mystic doctrines (see *The Gnostic Crucifixion*, pp. 40 ff.), was figured as the Fruit of the Fire-Tree. The Church Father Hippolytus (*Ref.*, vi. 9) summarizes the original text as follows:

" And, generally, we may say, of all things that are, both sensible and intelligible, which he [the writer of the *Announcement*] calls Manifested and Hidden, the Fire which is above the Heavens, is the Treasure, as it were a Great Tree, like that seen by Nebuchadonosor in vision, from which all flesh is nourished. And he considers the manifested side of the Fire to be the trunk, branches, leaves, and the bark surrounding it on the outside. All the parts of the Great Tree, he says, are set on fire by the devouring flame of the Fire and destroyed. But the Fruit of the Tree, if its imaging hath been perfected, and it takes the shape of itself, is placed in the Storehouse, and not cast into the Fire. For the Fruit, he says, is produced to be placed in the Storehouse, but the husk to be committed to the Fire; that is to say, the trunk which is generated not for its own sake but for that of the Fruit."

See further my *Simon Magus* (p. 14). The original form of this *Great Announcement* is in all probability a pre-Christian document (see *H.*, 184, n. 4), for the early Jewish commentator in the Naassene Document is acquainted with it. Now in this Document the pre-Christian Hellenistic initiate writes:

" Moreover, also, the Phrygians say that the Father of Wholes is Amygdalos [*lit.*, the Almond-Tree]."

And this is glossed by the same Jewish commentator, who knew *The Great Announcement*, as follows:

" No ordinary tree; but that He is that Amygdalos the Pre-existing, who, having in Himself the Perfect Fruit, as it were, throbbing and moving in His Depth, tore asunder His Womb, and gave birth to His own Son " (*H.*, i. 182).

THE PÆAN OF THE SOUL.

But to return to the Oracles ; Proclus evidently bases himself upon a very similar passage to the last-quoted verses of our poem, when he writes :

" Let us then offer this praise-giving to God—the becoming - like - unto - Him. Let us leave the Flowing Essence [the River of Genesis] and draw nigh to the true End ; let us get to know the Master, let all our love be poured forth to the Father. When He calls us, let us be obedient ; let us haste to the Hot, and flee the Cold ; let us be Fire ; let us ' fare on our *Way through Fire*.' We have an ' *agile Way* ' for our Return. ' *Our Father is our Guide*,' who ' *openeth the Ways of Fire*,' lest in forgetfulness we let ourselves flow in a ' *downward stream* ' " (K. 54).

The lust of generation is said to **THE CHALDÆAN ORACLES.** "moisten" the soul and make it watery; the Fire dries it and lightens it. The Hymn, or Praise-giving, which the souls sing on their Way Above is called by Olympiodorus, quoting most probably from the text of our poem, the "*Pæan*," or Song of Joy (C. 85); it is a continual praise-giving of the man who tunes himself into harmony with the Music of the Spheres. (See *The Hymns of Hermes*, pp. 17 ff., and 57 ff).

THE MYSTERY-CULTUS.

The cultus of the Oracles is, before all else, the cult of Fire, and that, too, for the most part, in a high mystical sense rather than in the cruder form of external fire-worship. The Sacred Living Fire was to be adored in the shrine of the silence of the inner nature. These inner mysteries were in themselves inexpressible, and even the very method of approach, it seems, was handed on under the vow of silence.

Our poem was thus originally intended to be an apocryphon (in the original sense of the term), or esoteric document ; for Proclus tells us that its mystagogy was prefaced by the words :

K. 55.
C. 51.
Keep silence, thou who art admitted to the secret rites [mýsta].

And elsewhere he says that the Oracles were handed on to the Mystæ alone. As a way of approach to the innermost form of the rites, which was indubitably a solitary sacrament like the *dynamis* of the *Mithriac Ritual*, there was an inner ceremonial cultus. Thus from one fragment we recover the following instruction to the officiating priest :

K. 55.
C. 193.
But, first of all, the priest who doth direct the Works of Fire, must sprinkle with cold wave of the deep-sounding brine.

There was, therefore, a ceremonial ritual. The consummation of the innermost rite, however, was solitary, and of the nature of a Mystic Union or Sacred Marriage.

THE CHALDÆAN ORACLES.

THE MYSTIC MARRIAGE.

Thus Proclus speaks of the soul, "according to a certain ineffable at-one-ment, leading that-which-is-filled into sameness with that-which-fills, making one portion of itself, in an immaterial and impalpable fashion, a receptacle for the in-shining, and provoking the other to the imparting of its Light." This, he says, is the meaning of the verse:

When the currents mingle in consummation of the Works of Deathless Fire. K. 55. C. 21.

THE PURIFYING MYSTERIES.

But this can be accomplished only in the perfected body, or rather "perfect body"; therefore, with regard to visions of the lower powers, operated by the daimones, Proclus tells us:

"The Gods admonish us not to look

THE CHALDÆAN ORACLES. upon them before we are fenced round with the powers brought to birth by the Mystery-rites:"

K. 55.
C. 150.
Thou should'st not look on them before the body is perfected; [for] ever do they fascinate men's souls and draw them from the Mysteries.

The lower visions were to be turned from in order that the higher theophanies, or manifestations of the Gods, might be seen. But this could be accomplished only by an orderly discipline. And so Proclus writes:

"For in contemplation and the art of perfectioning, that which makes the Way Above safe and free from stumbling-blocks for us, is orderly progress. At any rate, as the Oracles say:"

K. 56.
C. 183.
Never so much is God estranged from man, and, with Living Power, sends him on fruitless quests—

" As when, in disorder and in discord, we [try to] make the Ascent to the most divine heights of contemplation or the most sacred acts of Works—as it is said, '*with lips unhallowed and unwashen feet.*' "

THE CHALDÆAN ORACLES.

THE FIRE-GNOSIS.

Proclus further tells us that the first preliminary of this truly sacred cultus is that we should have a right intuition of the nature of the Divine, or, in the graphic words of the Oracles, a "*Fire-warmed intuition*" (K. 56) :

For if the mortal draw nigh to the Fire, he shall have Light from God.

K. 53.
C. 158.

There must, however, be no rush or hurry, but calm steadfast perseverance, for it is all a natural growth. Therefore is it said that :

For the mortal man who takes due time the Blessed Ones are swift to come into being.

K. 56.
C. 158.

THE CHALDÆAN ORACLES. This, however, does not mean to say that the man should be slow; for:

K. 56. *A mortal sluggish in these things spells the dismissal of the Gods.*

This is explained by an interesting passage of Damascius, who, speaking of the mysterious "instrument" the *iynx*, writes: "When it turns inwards, it invokes the Gods; and when outwards, it dismisses those it has invoked." Mystically this seems to mean that when the "whirl"—or vortex "instrument" of consciousness, or the one-sense "perfect body"—turns inwards, theophanies, or manifestations of the Gods, appear; and when it turns outward, to the physical, they disappear.

THE MANIFESTATIONS OF THE GODS.

In themselves the Gods have no forms, they are incorporeal; they, however, assume forms for the sake of mortals, as Proclus writes: "For though we [the Gods] are incorporeal:"   THE CHALDÆAN ORACLES.

Bodies are allowed to our self-revealed manifestations for your sakes.   K. 56. C. 106.

This self-revelation, which in one mode signifies the selection of some image in the seer's own mind, and in another, connotes the seeing by one's own light, pertains to the mystery of that monadic Light which transcends the three lower (empyrean, ætherial and hylic) planes or states (K. 31). And Simplicius further informs us (K. 57), quoting from Proclus:
"This, he says, is the Light which first receives the invisible allotments of the Gods, and for those worthy makes manifest in itself the self-revealed spectacles. For in it, he says, according to the Oracle:"

The things that have no shape, take shape.   K. 57. C. 114.

This seems to be the Astral Light

THE CHALDÆAN ORACLES. proper, "cosmic" and not personal. To this interpretation of Proclus', however, Simplicius objects that, according to the Oracles, the impressions of typical forms, or root-symbols, and of the other divine visions, do not occur in the Light, but are rather made on the æther (C. 113). We, however, need not labour the point further than to remark that Proclus had wider personal experience of those things than Simplicius. The things seen in the Great Light were true, for this Light constituted the Plane of Truth, whereas the æthereal was a reflection, and was further conditioned by the personality of the seer. Proclus, therefore, tells us that:

"The Gods [*i.e.*, presumably the Oracles] warn us to have understanding of '*the form of light that they display*'" (K. 57, C. 159).

In another passage Proclus refers to the mystic experience of these theophanies on the empyrean plane, where shapes of fire are assumed: "The tradition of these [visions] is handed on THE CHALDÆAN ORACLES. by the mystagogy of the tradition of the Gods; for it says:"

When thou hast uttered these [? words of power], thou shalt behold either a fire [? flame] resembling a boy, dancing upon the surface of the waves of air [? æther]; or even a flame that hath no shape, from which a voice proceeds; or [yet] a wealth of light around the area [of sight], strident, a-whirl. Nay, thou shalt see a horse as well, all made of fire, a-flash with light; or yet again a boy, on a swift horse's back astride,—a boy clad all in flame, or all bedecked with gold, or else with nothing on; or even shooting with a bow, and standing on horse-back.

K. 57.
C. 198.

With the above may be compared the symbolic visions in *A Mithriac Ritual* (pp. 27, 32); we have here evidently to do with the same order of experiences, and so also in the following four verses:

K. 57. *If thou should'st oft address Me, thou*
C. 196. *shalt behold all things grow dark; for at that hour no Heaven's curved dome is seen; there shine no Stars; Moon's light is veiled; Earth is no longer firm; with Lightning-flash all is a-flame.*

In connection with the idea underlying the phrase " a flame that hath no shape, from which a voice proceeds," of the last fragment but one, we must take the lines:

K. 58. *But when thou dost behold the very*
C. 199. *sacred Fire with dancing radiance flashing formless through the depths of the whole world, then hearken to the Voice of Fire.*

THE THEURGIC ART.

But to reach this pure and formless vision was very difficult; for all kinds of false appearances and changing shapes could intervene. These had to be cleaned from the field of vision, for they were held to be due to impure presences, or, as we should prefer it, to the impurities of the man's own lower nature. On this subject our Oracles (though more probably it is an interpolation from a Theurgic tradition) had instruction, as we learn from the curious fragment:

But when thou dost perceive an earthward daimon drawing nigh, make offering with the stone mnouziris, *uttering* [*the proper chant*].

K. 58.
C. 196.

What this stone may have been, we have no knowledge. To "make offering" with a stone can mean nothing else than to put it into the fire, and this should connect with alchemy. *Mnouziris* is a *barbarum nomen*.

The chant, or *mantra*, would also consist of *barbara nomina* (native names), concerning which Psellus quotes the famous lines that are generally referred to our Oracles, but which, for reasons of metre, could not have stood as part of the poem (C. 155):

THE CHALDÆAN ORACLES.

"See that thou never change the native names; for there are names in every nation, given by the Gods, possessed of power, in mystic rites, no language can express."

In this Theurgy, or "Divine Work," moreover, certain symbols, or symbolic figures, were employed, for Proclus says (K. 58) that the Oracles " call the angular points of the figures '*the compactors*.' "

THE ROYAL SOULS.

But Theurgy was not for all; it was the Royal Art, and could be practised with spiritual success only by those whom the Trismegistic writers (*H.*, iii. 125) would have called Royal Souls. Their nature is set forth in the following verses, preserved by Synesius:

K. 58.
C. 86.

Yea, verily, indeed, do they at least, most happy far of all the souls, pour down to Earth from Heaven; most blest are they with fates [lit., *threads*] *no tongue can tell, as many as are born from out*

Thy Radiant Self, O King, and from the Seed of Zeus Himself, through strong Necessity. — THE CHALDÆAN ORACLES.

This is evidently a reference to the Race, the Sons of God. (See *The Gnostic Crucifixion*, pp. 48 ff.). So also does the Orphic initiate declares : " My Race is from Heaven."

There may be some slight doubt as to whether the above fragment is from our poem, for Synesius does not say from what source he takes his quotation ; but short of the precise statement everything is in favour of its authenticity, and especially the following from the same philosophic and mystical Bishop :

THE LIGHT-SPARK.

"Let him hear the sacred Oracles which tell about the different ways. After the full list of inducements [or promptings] that come from Home to cause us to return, according to which it is within our power to cause the

márgin: THE CHALDÆAN ORACLES.
K. 59.
C. 165.

inplanted Seed to grow, they continue:"

To some He gave it to receive the Token of the Light, to others, even when asleep, He gave the power of bearing Fruit from His own Might.

The "Token of Light" is evidently the "Symbol" that the Father implants in souls. It is the Seed of Divinity, the Light-spark, that gradually flames forth into the Fire. This Light-spark was conceived of as a seed sown in good soil that could bear fruit, thirty, or sixty or a hundred fold, as the Christianized Gnosis has it.

And so in the Excerpts from the lost work of the Christian Gnostic Theodotus, made by the Church Father Clement of Alexandria, we read (K. 59): "The followers of the Valentinian doctrine declare that when the Psychic Body hath been enformed, into the Elect Soul in sleep the Masculine Seed is implanted by the Logos."

If the soul can pronounce its own true Word (Logos), utter its Sound, and so create by itself symbols, then may the man hope really to understand what his consciousness may catch from the highest spheres. But even if his soul cannot do this, even while it is unaware of its surroundings, and without this creative power, it is still possible that it may be able to catch some of the Strength and Might (not Light) of the Father-Mind, and thus be inspired to conceive some true ideas.

THE CHALDÆAN ORACLES.

The re-generated soul is said to become a " Five-fold Star," as we learn from the *Mithriac Ritual* (p. 24), and also from Lydus (*De Mens.*, 23.6), who tells us that : " The Oracle declares that souls, when restored to their former nature by means of this Pentad, transcend Fate."

For Theurgists are not counted in the herd subject to Fate.

K. 59.
C. 185.

And so also Proclus tells us that :

THE CHALDÆAN ORACLES.

" We should avoid the multitude of men that go '*in herds*,' as says the Oracle."

The "herd" has, so to speak, got only one "over-soul" between them,—they do not yet stand alone; or, rather, they have a soul each, and only one "over-mind" between them.

Those of the "herd" are the "processions of Fate" of the Trismegistic writings (*H*., iii. 273); while those who have perfected themselves, are freed from the Wheel of Fate, and become Angels or Gods. Speaking of the man who is truly devoted to sacred things, Proclus quotes an Oracle which says:

K. 60.   *Alive in power he runs, an Angel.*

THE UNREGENERATE.

On the contrary, the unregenerate is characterized as:

K. 60.   *Hard to turn, with burden on the back, who has no share in Light.*

While concerning those who " lead an evil life," Proclus tells us that the Oracles declared : *THE CHALDÆAN ORACLES.*

For as for them they are no great way off from Dogs irrational.　K. 60.

Of such a one it is said :

My vessel the Beasts of the Earth shall inhabit.　K. 60.
　　　C. 95.

Compare with this the Gnostic Valentinian doctrine, as summarized by Hippolytus :

" And this material man is, according to them, as it were an inn, or dwelling-place, at one time of the soul alone, at another of the soul and daimonian existences, at another of the soul and words (*logoi*), which are words sown from Above—from the Common Fruit of the Plērōma (Fulness) and Wisdom—into this world, dwelling in the body of clay together with the soul, when daimons cease to cohabit with her" (*F.*, p. 352).

And also the Basilidian doctrine, as summarized by Clement of Alexandria:

"The Basilidians are accustomed to give the name of appendages [or accretions] to the passions. These essences, they say, have a certain substantial existence, and are attached to the rational soul, owing to a certain turmoil and primitive confusion.

"Onto this nucleus other bastard and alien natures of the essence grow, such as those of the wolf, ape, lion, goat, etc. And when the peculiar qualities of such natures appear round the soul, they cause the desires of the soul to become like to the special natures of these animals, for they imitate the actions of those whose characteristics they bear" (*F.*, pp. 276, 277).

THE PERFECTING OF THE BODY.

The physical body was called in the Oracles the "dung of matter," as we have seen above (p. 38), and as we may see from the obscure couplet :

Thou shalt not leave behind the dung of matter on the height; the image [eidōlon] *also hath its portion in the space that shines on every side.*

K. 61.
C. 147.

This seems to mean either that the higher states of consciousness were not to be contaminated and befouled with the passions of the body, or that in the highest theurgy the body was not to be left behind in trance, but, on the contrary, that conscious contact was to be kept with it throughout the whole of the sacred operation, as we learn from the *Mithriac Ritual*. The "image" also—presumably the image-man, or subtle vehicle of the soul, the *augoeidēs* or *astroeidēs*—had an important part to play in linking the consciousness up with the Light-world.

In this connection we may also take the lines already quoted above (p. 58) :

K. 54. *If thou dost stretch thy fiery mind unto*
C. 176. *the flowing work of piety, thou shalt pre-*
serve thy body too.

What the "flowing work of piety" may be, it is hazardous to say. It is probably a poetical expression for the pure plastic substance out of which the "perfect body" was to be formed, as set forth in the *Mithriac Ritual*. The work of the "fiery mind" is thus described in the Trismegistic sermon "The Key":

"For when the soul withdraws into itself, the spirit doth contract itself within the blood, and soul within the spirit. And then the mind, stript of its wrappings, and naturally divine, taking unto itself a fiery body, doth traverse every space" (*H.*, ii. 151).

And again:

"When mind becomes a daimon, the law requires that it should take a fiery body to execute the services of God" (*H.*, ii. 154).

And here we may append a passage

from Julian the Emperor-Philosopher, who loved our Oracles :   THE CHALDÆAN ORACLES.

" To this the Oracles of the Gods bear witness ; and [therefore] I say that, by means of the holy life of purity, not only our souls but also our bodies are made worthy to receive much help and saving [or soundness] ; for they declare : "

Save ye as well the mortal thing of bitter matter that surrounds you.   K. 61.
C. 178.

For the mystery-term " bitter matter " see the note in the *Mithriac Ritual* (pp. 41 ff.). Kroll thinks that all this refers to the dogma of the resurrection of the physical body, but the Ritual makes it plain that the only " body of resurrection " with which the Mystics and Gnostics were acquainted, was the " perfect body"; the resurrection of the gross physical body was a superstition of the ignorant.

The " dung of matter " referred to above may be rendered as " dross " or

THE CHALDÆAN ORACLES.

"scum," and a somewhat more mystical interpretation might be suggested. "Dross" as a mystery-word is essentially the same as "scum," but from an analytical point of view suggests the reverse of "scum." Certain states of the soul may be spoken of as scum; in spiritual alchemy when the soul-plasm is thought of as the "watery" sphere being gradually dried, so as to be eventually built up, or enformed, by the "fire" of the spiritual mind, then the scum rises to the top and is handed over to Fate. Scum would then mean men under the bondage of Fate. Dross, however, suggests the earth or metal side of things, and here the refuse falls and does not rise, and is again handed over to further schooling and discipline, and not allowed freedom from the law, like jewels and pure earth are.

Scum and dross are on the matter-side of things; images may be said to correspond to them on the mind-side. As scum is to the soul, as dross to pure matter, so is image to pure mind. Both scum and image have to do with the surface of things and not with the depth.

RE-INCARNATION.

As we might expect, the Oracles taught the doctrine of the repeated descents and returnings of the soul, by whatever name we may call it, whether transmigration, re-incarnation, palingenesis, metempsychosis, metensomatosis, or transcorporation. And so Proclus tells us that:

"They make the soul descend many times into the world for many causes, either through the shedding of its feathers [or wings], or by the Will of the Father" (K. 62).

The soul of a man, however, as also in the Trismegistic doctrine (*H.*, ii. 153, 166), could not be reborn into the body of a brute; as to this Proclus is quite clear when he writes:

"And that the passing into irrational natures is contrary to nature for human souls, not only do the Oracles teach us,

<small>THE CHALDÆAN ORACLES.</small> when they declare that '*this is the law from the Blessed Ones that naught can break*'; the human soul:"

K. 62.   *Completes its life again in men and not in beasts.*

THE DARKNESS.

There was also in our Oracles a doctrine of punishment in the Invisible (Hadēs); for Proclus speaks of "the Avenging Powers (*Poinaí*), '*Throttlers of mortals*,'" and of a state of gloom and pain, below which stretched a still more awful gulf of Darkness, as the following verses tell us:

K. 62.
C. 145.   *See that thou verge not down unto the world of the Dark Rays, 'neath which is ever spread the Deep* [or *Abyss*] *devoid of form, where is no light to see, wrapped in black gloom befouling, that joys in shades* [eidōla], *void of all understanding, precipitous and sinuous, for ever winding*

round its own blind depth, eternally in marriage with a body that cannot be seen, inert [and] lifeless.

With this description of the Serpent of Darkness, ever in congress with his infernal counterpart of blind Matter and Ignorance, may be compared the vision of the Trismegistic " Man-Shepherd " treatise :

" But in a little while Darkness came settling down on part of it, awesome and gloomy, coiling in sinuous folds, so that methought it like unto a snake " (*H.*, ii. 4.).

This is a vision of the other side, or antipodes, of the Light ; and so we find Proclus writing : " For this region is '*Hater of the Light*,' as the Oracle also saith " (K. 63). Also with regard to the system thought to underlie the Oracles, Psellus informs us that below the Æther come three hylic worlds or planes of gross matter—the sublunary, terrene, and sub-terrene—" the uttermost of which is

THE CHALDÆAN ORACLES. called chthonian and '*Light-hater*,' and is not only sublunary, but also contains within it that matter (*hylē*) which they call the '*Deep*.'"

THE INFERNAL STAIRS.

In connection with the above fragment we must also take the following corrupt lines, which evidently form part of the directions given to the soul for its journey through Hades:

K. 63.
C. 159.
But verge not downwards! Beneath thee lies a Precipice, sheer from the earth, that draws one down a Stair of seven steps, beneath which lies the Throne of Dire Necessity.

The topography of the Throne of Necessity corresponds somewhat with that in Plato's famous Vision of Er—which was probably derived from an Orphic mystery-myth; and the old Orphic tradition was in contact with "Chalddæan" sources. So also in the Vision of Aridæus, which again is perhaps connected with Orphic initiation, it is Adrasteia, Daughter of Necessity, who presides over the punishments in Tartarus, and her dominion extends to the uttermost parts of the hylic cosmos, as we learn from a fragment of a theogony preserved by Jerome (K. 63).

Proclus also speaks of the whole generative or genesiurgic Nature—that is, Nature under the sway of Necessity—in which, he says, is "both the '*turbulence of matter*' and the '*light-hating world*,' as the Gods [*i.e.*, the Oracles] say, and the '*sinuous streams*,' by which the many are drawn down, as the Oracles tell us."

Moreover, there must have been mention of some roaring or bellowing sound that struck the evil soul with terror, as in the Vision of Er; for Psellus quotes a mutilated fragment, which runs:

"*Ah! Ah!*" *the Earth doth roar at them, until* [*they turn*] *to children* (?).   K. 63.

THE CHALDÆAN ORACLES.

We may, however, venture to suggest another point of view from which the above symbolic imagery (K. 62) can be regarded, and take it not as a warning to ordinary fate-full people, but as an admonition to those who are being initiated or re-generated, and who can thus begin to stand aside from the Fate-spheres.

The "Precipice," or Gulph, could thus be regarded as the way of descent from the Light and the Fulness into the Fate-spheres, and so the organ or instrument of creation of darkness and "flat" things (shades). The soul descends by means of a "flat" ladder of planes, the way of the formal mind.

The admonition thus seems to say: Do not let the mind travel down into the Fate-spheres by means of "planes" and formal ideas, and the ordinary surface view of things; because if so, it is apt to leave some of itself behind. There is a way of descending direct and straight into, or rather fathoming, the uttermost

Depths quite safely, but it is by way of living creatures, and not by way of mind-made ladders.

In mystical language "Throne" is the point of stability: it suggests contact with the Stable One. This plan of seven, the ladder or root of form, is essentially stable and not vital; and for an initiate who is on the return journey, active in the mystery of re-generation, it is to be avoided, as it leads back into imprisonment; it is the proper way down, but not the right way back. It leads to states dominated by Fate, to a prison or school where the soul is bound all round with rules; it does not lead to Freedom.

ON CONDUCT.

We may now conclude with some fragments concerning right living; in the first place with the famous riddle:

Soil not the spirit, and deepen not the plane!

K. 64.
C. 152.

THE CHALDÆAN ORACLES.

The first clause is generally thought to refer to the spiritual, or rather spirituous, body, while the second is supposed to mean: "Turn not the plane into the solid"—that is to say, if we follow Pythagoræan tradition: Do not make the subtle body dense or gross.

From a more mystical point of view it might be suggested that normal Nature is but as a superficies. Until a man is initiated properly, that is to say, naturally re-generated, it is better for him not to delve into her magical powers too soon, but rather keep within the plane-side of things till his own substance is made pure. When pure there is nothing in him to which these magical powers can attach themselves. As soon as his nature is purified then Spiritual Mind begins to enter his "perfect body," and so he can control the inner forces, or forces within, or sexual powers of Nature — those creative powers and passions which make her double herself. The superficial side of Nature is complete in its own way, and normal man should be content with this; he should not attempt to stir the secret powers of her Depth, or Womb, till he is guided by the wisdom of the Spiritual Mind.

THE CHALDÆAN ORACLES.

In the Latin translation of Proclus' lost treatise *On Providence*, the following three sayings are ascribed to the Oracles (*Responsa*). Kroll, however, thinks that the second only is authentic:

When thou dost look upon thyself, let fear come on thee.

K. 64.
C. 181.

Believe thyself to be out of body, and thou art.

The spawning of illnesses in us is in our own control, for they are born out of the life we lead.

If the man regards his own lower self, he fears because of his imperfection; if he gazes on his higher self, he feels awe.

With the second aphorism compare

THE CHALDÆAN ORACLES.

the instruction of the Trismegistic treatise "The Mind to Hermes" (§ 19):

"And, thus, think from thyself, and bid thy soul go unto any land, and there more quickly than thy bidding will it be" (*H.*, ii. 186).

THE GNOSIS OF PIETY.

That the spirit of the doctrine of the Oracles was far removed from the practice of the arts of astrology, earth-measurement, divination, augury, and the rest, and turned the mind to the contemplation of spiritual verities alone, may be seen from the following fine fragment:

K. 64.
C. 144.

Submit not to thy mind the earth's vast measures, for that the Tree of Truth grows not on earth; and measure not the measure of the sun by adding rod to rod, for that his course is in accordance with the Will eternal of the Father, and not for sake of thee. Let thou the moon's rush go; she ever runs by operation of

K. 34.　　*Both lunar course and star-progression.*
C. 144.　　*This star-progression was not delivered from the womb of things because of thee.*

K. 56.　　*Bodies are allowed our self-revealed*
C. 186.　　*manifestations for your sakes.*

And so we bring these two small volumes to a close in the hope that a few at least of the many riddles connected with these famous Oracles may have been made somewhat less puzzling.